How to Use Credit

Ryan Randolph

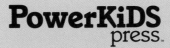
PowerKiDS press.

New York

Published in 2014 by The Rosen Publishing Group, Inc.
29 East 21st Street, New York, NY 10010

First Edition

Editor: Jennifer Way
Book Design: Greg Tucker

Photo Credits: Cover Morgan Lane Photography/Shutterstock.com; p. 4 MJTH/Shutterstock.com; p. 5 Hemera Technologies/PhotoObjects.net/Thinkstock; p. 6 Losevsky Photo and Videos/Shutterstock.com; p. 7 Image Source/ Getty Images; pp. 8–9 Brand X Pictures/Thinkstock; p. 10 Andresr/Shutterstock.com; p. 11 Jack Hollingsworth/ Photodisc/Thinkstock; p. 12 Wavebreak Media/Thinkstock; p. 13 Michael Nagle/Getty Images; p. 14 Multiart/ Shutterstock.com; p. 15 (top) Hemera/Thinkstock; p. 15 (bottom) Stockbyte/Thinkstock; p. 16 AISPIX by Image Source/Shutterstock.com; p. 17 Digital Vision/Thinkstock; pp. 18–19 iStockphoto/Thinkstock; p. 20 Jupiterimages/ Comstock/Thinkstock; p. 21 Stuart Miles/Shutterstock.com; p. 22 Neyro/Shutterstock.com.

Library of Congress Cataloging-in-Publication Data

Randolph, Ryan P.
 How to use credit / by Ryan Randolph. — 1st ed.
    p. cm. — (A smart kid's guide to personal finance)
 Includes index.
 ISBN 978-1-4777-0744-9 (library binding) — ISBN 978-1-4777-0829-3 (pbk.) —
 ISBN 978-1-4777-0830-9 (6-pack)
 1. Consumer credit—Juvenile literature. 2. Credit cards—Juvenile literature. I. Title.
 HG3755.R36 2014
 332.7'43—dc23
                                        2012044926

Manufactured in the United States of America

CPSIA Compliance Information: Batch #S13PK5: For Further Information contact Rosen Publishing, New York, New York at 1-800-237-9932

Contents

Using Credit

Have you ever seen your parents use a **credit card** at the store? They swipe a card, sign a paper, and walk off with what they bought. No cash was given, so how did they pay?

When a credit card is swiped, the store is paid electronically for the purchase.

Using a credit card is a way to pay for things without handing over cash directly. Using credit is different from using cash. Using credit is **borrowing** money from another place, such as a bank. This money must be paid back at a later date. It costs money to borrow this money, so it is important to use credit carefully. Learning to use credit wisely is an important money skill.

Have you ever asked for an advance on your allowance? That's a little bit like asking your parents for credit.

What Is Credit?

People often use credit cards when they travel because it is easier to carry cards instead of cash.

When a person uses credit, she is borrowing money. The bank or credit card company pays for what the person bought. Then she pays back the bank or credit card company.

It costs money to use credit. The amount of money it costs is called **interest**. It is often shown as a percent, like 15%. People like to use credit because they can buy things now and pay over time. It can also be safer and easier to use a credit card than to carry cash for large purchases. Banks and credit card companies like giving credit because they earn money from the interest they collect.

When people buy an expensive item, such as a new TV, they might use a credit card so they do not have to bring lots of cash to the store.

Ways to Pay

People can pay for things in several ways. They may use cash, checks, **debit cards**, and credit cards.

Cash, checks, and debit cards are ways of paying with money you already have. A debit card looks like a credit card, but it is different. The store is paid money directly from your bank account. With a credit card, the store is paid money from the bank or credit card company. Each month the bank or credit card company sends a bill that lists what was bought with that credit card. Then the person pays back that money, with any interest that has been added.

When people pay for something in cash, they have to have the full amount needed right then.

Reaching Goals with Credit

Many students take out loans to pay for college. They then pay back the loan over several years after they finish school.

Credit cards are not the only way that people use credit. People use credit in the form of loans to reach big goals, such as buying a car or house or paying for a college education.

A loan for a house is called a **mortgage**. Mortgages allow people to live in a house while paying back the loan for it. They make monthly mortgage payments, which are for the amount they borrowed, with interest. It is important that borrowers pay back their mortgage. If a borrower cannot pay the mortgage, the bank will take back the house in place of the borrowed money. This process is called **foreclosure**.

Houses are expensive. It would take most people many years to save up enough money to pay for a house in full. Mortgages help more people afford to buy homes.

Good Things About Credit

When you use credit, you can get things you want or need immediately and pay for them over time. Things like houses, cars, and college would be difficult or impossible for most people to pay for all at once. Credit makes these big goals affordable to more people.

Most online purchases are made using credit cards.

Credit cards can be helpful tools. People can buy things without carrying lots of cash. They allow people to shop online. Credit cards can help people keep track of their spending because the bill shows where, when, and how much they spent. If they pay their monthly bill in full, the credit they use does not cost them any interest.

Many credit card companies offer purchase protection. This helps the consumer if what she purchased is broken, lost, or stolen within a certain time after the purchase.

Risks of Abusing Credit

If a person makes a late payment or skips a payment, he will be charged a fee. This fee is called a penalty.

It is important to use credit wisely. Imagine you buy a bike for $100 using a credit card. If you pay back the $100 when the bill comes, then no interest is charged. A credit card bill shows the amount you owe, as well as the **minimum** amount you must pay.

If a person falls behind on her payments for a car loan, her car might get taken back by the bank. This is called repossession.

Interest is charged on the **balance** until it is paid back, though. This means your bike could end up costing you much more than $100.

People can get in trouble abusing credit. If they make late payments, they are charged fees as punishment. Owing money is called **debt**. If people cannot pay off their debt, they may go **bankrupt**.

If a person borrows more money than she can afford to pay back, whether through credit cards or loans, she could end up going bankrupt. People usually have to go to court to declare bankruptcy.

What Is a Credit Score?

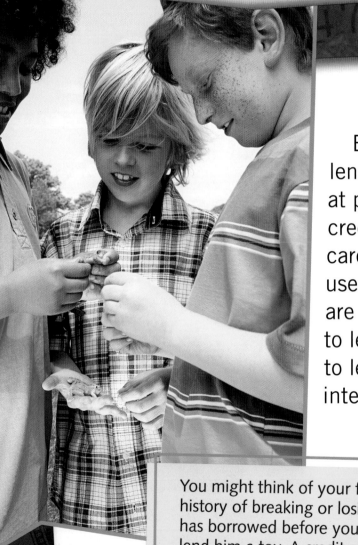

Banks decide whom to lend money to by looking at people's **credit scores**. A credit score is like a report card of how well a person uses credit. Credit scores are used to decide whether to lend money, how much to lend, and how much interest to charge.

You might think of your friend's history of breaking or losing toys he has borrowed before you decide to lend him a toy. A credit score works in a similar way to grade a person's money-borrowing history.

AL TENDER
IC AND PRIVATE

Those with low credit scores may be loaned less and have to pay more interest. Those with really bad scores may not be able to get credit at all! Taking out credit is important in starting a credit score. Paying credit card and other bills on time helps a credit score. Not paying bills on time hurts a credit score.

People sometimes ask for printed copies of their credit scores, called credit reports. They can see what their scores are and if there are any mistakes in the reports.

The Fine Print Matters!

Banks want to make it easy to use credit. They often make it difficult to understand how much it costs, though. Consumers have to look carefully at the terms, or rules, of the credit they are being offered. This is called looking at the fine print.

Consumers need to shop around before choosing to take out credit. For example, different banks and credit card companies may offer different interest rates. Finding a lower interest rate is good, but look at the fine print! Sometimes a low interest rate goes up after a period of time.

Banks and credit card companies send detailed information about their terms. This is called the fine print because these rules are often written in very small type!

Using Credit Wisely

Ask your parents to talk to you about financial responsibility. They may have good advice and be able to help you find more information.

Financial responsibility means using money wisely. Examples of financial responsibility include not spending more money than you have, saving for a rainy day, and using credit carefully.

The cost of using credit is more than just the cost of the purchase and the interest. When people abuse credit today, they may find it harder or impossible to get credit in the future. That means they might have trouble getting a mortgage for a house in their 30s because they were not financially responsible in their 20s. Thinking about using credit means thinking about how to pay it back and how that can affect you years from now.

Some parents give their kids access to their credit card or give them special credit cards for young adults. This is meant to teach them to use credit wisely, not to go shopping!

Smart Credit Tips

1. You cannot get your own credit card until you are an adult. There are online games that teach smart credit habits, though. They let you practice making good choices.

2. Credit cards are private. That means that people cannot use someone else's card. It also means people should never share their credit card numbers.

3. Pay more than the minimum amount required of any loan. The faster you pay off credit, the less the loan costs you in interest!

4. Pay credit card bills on time. On-time payment helps avoid late fees. Credit card interest rates can also jump if you do not pay bills on time!

5. Debit cards are great for purchases you can afford. The money is linked to a bank account. This allows people to use their money without carrying lots of cash around.

Glossary

balance (BAL-ens) The amount of money in a bank account.

bankrupt (BANGK-rupt) Unable to pay the debts one owes to others.

borrowing (BOR-oh-ing) Using something that belongs to someone else for a certain time.

credit card (KREH-dit KAHRD) A card used to buy something with an agreement to pay for it later.

credit scores (KREH-dit SKORZ) Numbers that decide whether and how much people should be lent money.

debit cards (DEH-but KAHRDZ) Cards used to pay for things or to take money out of accounts.

debt (DET) Something owed.

financial responsibility (fuh-NANT-shul rih-spont-suh-BIH-luh-tee) Using money wisely and well.

foreclosure (for-KLOH-zhur) When a bank takes back a property because the owner cannot make the mortgage payments.

interest (IN-teh-rest) The extra cost that someone pays in order to borrow money.

minimum (MIH-nih-mum) The smallest amount accepted.

mortgage (MAWR-gij) An agreement to use a building or piece of land as security for a loan. If the loan is not paid back, the lender gets to keep the building or land.

Index

Websites

Due to the changing nature of Internet links, PowerKids Press has developed an online list of websites related to the subject of this book. This site is updated regularly. Please use this link to access the list: www.powerkidslinks.com/skgpf/credit/

mL   12-13